Introduction

Now is the most exciting time to learn how to crochet! Never before has there been such a fabulous array of styles to crochet for you, your family, and your home. Even those projects designed especially for the beginner are stunning because of the wonderful variety of yarns that are available.

Learning to crochet will not only give you a feeling of great accomplishment and satisfaction but will help relieve the stress of living in our fast-paced world. Researchers have found that the repetitive movements of a needlecraft block the hormone noradrenaline, thus lowering your blood pressure and heart rate. The peaceful feeling you'll experience has often been

Crochet fits perfectly into a busy, giving you the opportunity to crochet while you pass the time waiting in the inevitable line, or traveling by car, bus, train or plane. A guilty pleasure like watching television becomes productive when you multitask with crochet. Just think, you can watch your favorite shows and make beautiful things to wear all at the same time!

So turn the page and take the first step on your wonderful journey to learning all about **crochet basics!**

Contents

Starter Projects

Get Hooked
Page 25

Double the Fun
Page 26

Pillow Talk
Page 26

Full Circle
Page 27

A Step Up
Page 28

Around the Clock
Page 29

Getting Started

Whether you've always wanted to learn how to crochet, need to brush up on forgotten skills, or are a knitter who's always had to pass on projects that were embellished with crochet, you've come to the right place!

I Can Crochet has all the information you need to know to make you a bona fide crocheter. Divided into three sections, this book takes you step by step through the entire learning process. The first section addresses everything from making basic stitches through increasing, decreasing, sewing seams, and other essential techniques that will send you on your way to making your first project.

Once you have a firm grasp on the basics, simply go on to the second section, which is filled with lots of wonderful projects for you to make to hone your newfound skills, not to mention to wear or give as gifts. Begin with quick and easy scarves that feature stitches and techniques you already know, then move on to hats, granny squares, and more! You'll find that each project gets a little more challenging by introducing a new skill or technique that will make you a well-rounded crocheter.

The third section shows you how to correct the two most common mistakes: having too many chain stitches or not having enough chain stitches. You'll also find everything you'll need to know about caring for your beautiful garments, from cleaning to storing so they'll last a lifetime.

Have fun on your journey to explore this wonderful and much-loved craft. So get yourself comfortable and read on!

Hooks

It's quite amazing that such a simple tool can do so much, considering it has no moving parts. Let's look at a crochet hook to get familiar with its five different sections.

The tip and the throat (the hook) are used to make a stitch; the diameter of the shaft section determines the size of the hook; and the grip and the handle are used to hold the hook.

Crochet hooks come in two classifications: yarn hooks and steel (or thread) hooks. Yarn hooks are designed specifically to be used with yarn. They are manufactured in manmade materials such as aluminum, plastic, and acrylic, or natural materials such as bamboo, abalone, bone, and hardwoods (birch, maple, rosewood, and ebony). Some are available with ergonomically shaped handles and comfort grips, as well as other special features. But as a beginner, you should opt for aluminum hooks first. They are easy to hold, inexpensive, durable, and readily

available. After you have a few projects under your belt, you may want to experiment with other types and styles to see if any suit you better.

Yarn crochet hook sizes are always listed from the smallest (used with thinner yarns) to the largest (used with thicker yarns). In the United States, hooks are sized by letters of the alphabet, except for the size 7. The number next to the letter is the equivalent knitting needle size. For most sizes, you'll find the size of the hook stamped on the grip.

Although only yarn hooks are used in this book, you might want to explore finer crochet projects someday, so it's a good idea to be familiar with steel hooks. Steel crochet hooks are designed to be used with certain types of crochet thread, such as cotton and linen. These hooks are always listed from the largest (used with thicker threads) to the smallest (used with finer threads). Note that unlike yarn hooks, the lower the number, the larger the hook. For this type of hook, the size can always be found on the grip.

Yarn

You'll be like a kid in a candy store when you step into a yarn shop. Never before has there been such a vast variety of gorgeous yarns to choose

from for every taste and budget. See all the wonderful natural fibers to explore like wool, mohair, alpaca, angora, cashmere, cotton, linen, and silk. Today's latest high-tech synthetics include the most affordable acrylics and the more pricey novelties like metallics, furs, and even yarn that looks and feels like suede!

Adding to the variety are the textures that abound, from smooth, classic plied yarns to loopy bouclés. Now multiply them all by the colors. Just about every solid color imaginable can be found—from clear brights to dusty pastels to rich earth tones—plus amazing multicolor yarns like tweed, variegateds (lengths of different colors alternated within the same ball), stripes, and more!

Yarn Weights

All yarns are classified by their weight (thickness of the yarn), no matter what fibers the yarns are made from. They range from superfine (the thinnest) to superbulky (the thickest). Each weight yarn has a recommended crochet hook size and a range of how many single crochet stitches you will get to the inch when you crochet using that size hook. This is called the *gauge* and it will be discussed in detail starting on page 14 The basic rule of thumb is that the finer the

YARN CROCHET HOOKS					
U.S.	Metric	U.S.	Metric	U.S.	Metric
B/1	2.25mm	H/8	5.00mm	P/16	12.00mm
C/2	2.75mm	I/9	5.50mm		
D/3	3.25mm	J/10	6.00mm		
E/4	3.50mm	K/10½	6.50mm		
F/5	3.75mm	L/11	8.00mm		
G/6	4.00mm	M/13	9.00mm		
7	4.50mm	N/15	10.00mm		

STEEL CROCHET HOOKS					
U.S.	Metric	U.S.	Metric	U.S.	Metric
00	3.50mm	5	1.90mm	11	1.10mm
0	3.25mm	6	1.80mm	12	1.00mm
1	2.75mm	7	1.65mm	13	.85mm
2	2.25mm	8	1.50mm	14	.75mm
3	2.10mm	9	1.40mm		
4	2.00mm	10	1.30mm		

throat   shaft   grip   handle

tip

yarn, the smaller the hook size, and the bulkier the yarn, the larger the hook size. However, there are always exceptions to the rule. There are lace patterns that call for a fine yarn and large hook to achieve a light and airy fabric. The chart on this page will help you familiarize yourself with what size hook to use with what weight yarn. This chart will always come in handy when choosing the right yarns and hooks for your projects.

Yarn Packaging

Yarn is available in three forms: pull-skein, pre-wound ball, and hank. To use a pull-skein, simply poke your fingers inside the center of the skein to find the end, then carefully pull it out. At first you might have to tug a bit to get the yarn to come out, but after a few yards have been used, the yarn should flow freely.

For a pre-wound ball, remove the paper label. To prevent the ball from rolling away while you work, you can contain it in two ways. You can place the ball in a plastic bag and either tape the bag to your worktable. Or pin it to the arm of your chair. Place the ball inside a plastic bag (to keep it clean) and place it in a work bag or basket that sits on the floor.

A hank must first be wound into a ball before you can use it. The easiest way to do it by hand is to have a helper. Remove the paper label and have the helper hold the hank fairly taut over outstretched hands. As you wind the yarn, the helper

Categories of yarn, gauge ranges, and recommended crochet hook sizes

Yarn Weight Symbol & Category Names	1 Super Fine	2 Fine	3 Light	4 Medium	5 Bulky	6 Super Bulky
Type of Yarns in Category	Sock, Fingering, Baby	Sport, Baby	DK, Light Worsted	Worsted, Afghan, Aran	Chunky, Craft, Rug	Bulky, Roving
Crochet Gauge Ranges in Single Crochet to 4 inch	21–32 sts	16–20 sts	12–17 sts	11–14 sts	8–11 sts	5–9 sts
Recommended Hook U.S. Size Range	B–1 to E–4	E–4 to 7	7 to I–9	I–9 to K–10½	K–10½ to M–13	M–13 and larger
Recommended Hook in Metric Size Range	2.25–3.5 mm	3.5–4.5 mm	4.5–5.5 mm	5.5–6.5 mm	6.5–9 mm	9–12 mm and larger

should move his or her hands back and forth, allowing the yarn to come off his or her hands one wrap at a time. Make sure to wind the ball loosely. Winding it too tight might cause the yarn to lose its elasticity. If you need to go it alone, you can place the hank around the back of one or two chairs (depending on the circumference of the hank) and wind it from there. Place the ball inside a plastic bag same as for a pre-wound ball.

Tip

Save the paper label! This little piece of paper (called a ball band) is packed with important information that you need to know before you begin a project and after you finish it. There's fiber content, color, dye lot, yardage/meters, ounces/grams, suggested hook size/gauge, and care instructions. And many pull-skein labels have free project directions, too!

First Steps to Stitches

What You'll Need

The best size crochet hook to start with is an H/8 (5mm) that is made of aluminum. This size is comfortable to hold in your hand, making the movements of crocheting easier than using a very small or very large hook.

To work with a size H/8 (5mm) hook, you will need 4-ply knitting worsted-weight yarn. You can opt for a synthetic fiber such as acrylic, a natural fiber such as wool, or one that is a blend like wool and nylon. For your first time out it's best to stay away from cotton, which is not as easy to crochet with as those just mentioned because it doesn't have a lot of elasticity. Choose a solid color that you like, but keep your choice light in tone. Keep in mind that stitches made using dark colors, like black and navy, are harder to see.

Hands-on Know-How

There are two ways you can hold a crochet hook. The first, and recommended, grip is like a knife.

1 The first and recommended grip is like a knife.

2 The second hold is like a pencil.

Position the hook in your hand so your thumb is flat on the front of the grip, your index finger is flat on the back of the grip, and the hook (tip and throat) is facing you. Secure the handle by wrapping your remaining fingers around it. It should feel comfortable in your hand. Practice the hold by putting the hook down, then picking it up again, positioning the hook as described, until it feels like second nature to you.

The second hold is like a pencil. Although you have the freedom to choose which way is

more comfortable for you, doctors have discovered that holding the hook like a pencil may cause carpal tunnel syndrome; that's why it's best to go with the knife hold.

Slip Knot

The slip knot is simply a way of tying the end of the yarn to create a loop that can be adjusted to fit the size of the crochet hook. This important little loop anchors the yarn to the hook so you can make a chain and then crochet stitches.

Hold on!

Before you make your first chain, it's time to learn how to hold the yarn in conjunction with holding the crochet hook. The hardest thing to remember here is to relax and breathe! The tighter you hold the yarn and hook, the harder it will be to work. It's all going to seem awkward at first, but try not to get frustrated. Soon it will become second nature to you—with a little practice.

Making a Foundation Chain

The foundation chain is the base for making all the crochet stitches you'll be learning how to do. It is simply a series of loops (called chain stitches) that are linked together. It's in these chain stitches that you will make the crochet stitches.

There are four important things to remember as you make a foundation chain:

1 It's all in the wrists. As you work, your arms should stay comfortably at your sides allowing your wrists to do most of the actions.

2 For each chain stitch, you'll be using about 1"/2.5cm worth of yarn, so let the yarn coming from the ball slide smoothly from under your pinkie and over your index finger every time you make a stitch. Don't forget that your index finger should always be about 1½"/4cm from the tip of the crochet hook.

3 Every time you've made four or five chain stitches, move your thumb and middle finger up and resecure the foundation chain by holding the last chain stitch made between these two fingers. Remember that your thumb and middle finger should never be more than 1½"/4cm from the tip of the crochet hook.

4 Stay relaxed and don't sweat it! If you make a mistake, simply start over.

SLIP KNOT

1 Reel off about a yard/meter of yarn from the ball. Hold the yarn in your palm with your thumb about 6"/15cm from the end. Using the yarn coming from the ball, wrap the yarn twice around your index and middle fingers.

2 Pull the strand coming from the ball through the loop between your two fingers, forming a new loop.

3 Place this new loop on the hook. Firm up the knot by pulling on the free end of the yarn. Now adjust the size of the loop by pulling on the yarn coming from the ball until it fits the hook but slides easily on the shaft.

HOLDING THE YARN

1 Hold the hook, with the slip knot attached, in your hand making sure the free end of the yarn is hanging down. Now hold the yarn coming from the ball in your other hand so the yarn goes halfway around your index finger (about 1½"/4cm from the base of the slip knot), then anchor the yarn with your pinky.

2 Secure the free end that's hanging down by holding the base of the slip knot between your thumb and middle finger. Now you're ready to make a chain!

MAKING A FOUNDATION CHAIN

1 To make each chain stitch, you need to wrap the yarn over the hook from the back to the front. To do this, keep your index finger straight and twist your wrist toward you. At the same time, twist your other wrist away from you to bring the yarn in front of the hook. Now twist both wrists back to their original positions. The yarn will now be caught under the hook. This is called a yarn over.

2 To draw the yarn through the loop on the hook, first twist your wrist toward you so the hook is facing down. Now pull the yarn through the loop, then twist your wrist back to its original position so the hook is facing you again. You have now made one chain stitch.

3 You might have to adjust the size of the loop on the hook so it slides easily and slightly loosely along the shaft. To make it larger, use the hook to pull up on the loop while allowing the extra yarn needed to feed off your index finger. To make it smaller, use your index finger to pull on the yarn until the loop is the right size. Continue to make chain stitches, adjusting the loop on the hook as you go so all the chain stitches are the same size.

Time to Crochet!

Anatomy of a Foundation Chain

Now that you know how to make a foundation chain, you need to know what the different parts of a chain are before you begin to crochet stitches.

A foundation chain has two sides. The side that faces you while you make the chain stitches is called the top. Along the top, the chain stitches form a line of "V"s. Each chain stitch "V" has two strands. The strand that is to the right (or nearest you) is called the front loop. The strand that is to the left (or farthest from you) is called the back loop. It is in these loops that you will make crochet stitches.

The side opposite the top is called the bottom. On the bottom, the chain stitches form a single line of "bumps." Examine them closely and you'll see that they are actually loops as well. These are called the bottom loops. Some projects will have you crochet into the bottom loops, but for now we will be referring only to the two top loops.

Counting Chain Stitches

Looking at the foundation chain, note that the loop that's on the hook is not counted as a chain stitch, nor is the slip knot. When you count the chain stitches, always count from the first stitch after the hook to the last stitch before the slip knot.

Why and Where

You will be learning how to do four basic crochet stitches. They range in height from the shortest to the tallest as follows: single crochet, half double crochet, double crochet, and treble crochet. Into which chain stitch you make your first crochet stitch depends on the height of the finished crochet stitch. One chain stitch equals the height of a single crochet stitch, so you will make

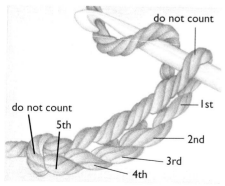
Counting chain stitches on a foundation chain

(image labels: do not count, do not count, 5th, 4th, 3rd, 2nd, 1st)

1 Insert the hook under both the front and back loops of the 2nd chain from the hook. (You can also use your other thumb to help it along.) Wrap the yarn over the hook from the back to the front (this is called a yarn over), then catch it with the hook. Now draw the hook through the two chain stitch loops. You now have two loops on the hook.

2 Wrap the yarn over the hook from the back to the front (yarn over), then draw the yarn over through both loops on the hook.

3 You have now completed one single crochet stitch. Continue to repeat Steps 1 and 2 nine more times, inserting the hook into each chain stitch across. You now have ten single crochet stitches completed across the row.

4 To proceed to the next row, make one chain stitch (this is the turning chain), then turn the piece from the right to the left; this step is called *chain and turn*. Remember that one chain stitch equals the height of the single crochet stitch and that you will always turn the piece from the right to the left. To begin the next row, insert the hook under both the front and back loops of the first stitch (skipping the one turning chain stitch). Continue to repeat the steps until you have completed ten rows of single crochet.

your first stitch in the 2nd chain stitch from the hook. Here, the 1st chain stitch (or the one that was skipped) is the one chain stitch needed to obtain the height. For a half double crochet, you need two chain stitches to equal the height, so you will make your first stitch in the 3rd chain stitch from the hook (skipping the 1st and 2nd chain stitches). Likewise, a double crochet begins in the 4th chain stitch (three chain stitches to equal the height) and the treble crochet begins in the 5th chain stitch (four chain stitches to equal the height).

Although it's good to know why and where you begin to crochet a stitch, you don't need to rely on your memory because directions for a pattern stitch will always state where to begin.

Single Crochet

The first row of any crochet stitch is the hardest. This is because you don't have a lot to hold on to, so it's always going to be a bit clumsy. Take it slow. Keep in mind that once you've completed the first row, the rest will go much easier.

To begin your first row of single crochet, make a foundation chain that has eleven chain stitches.

Hold the yarn and crochet hook as before. Now hold the foundation chain so the top is facing you and your thumb and middle finger are holding the 3rd chain stitch from the hook. To go onto a chain stitch easier, slide your thumb from the grip up to the throat of the hook, then anchor the loop on the hook with your thumb.

Fastening Off

When you have completed the number of rows called for or have achieved the length measurement stated in a direction, you need to secure the last stitch so the rest of the stitches don't come undone or unravel. This is called fastening off. Simply cut the yarn coming from the ball about 12"/30.5cm from the loop on the hook. Bring the yarn over the hook, then draw the yarn end (called a tail) all the way through the loop on the hook. Pull the tail to tighten and secure the last stitch.

FASTENING OFF

Half Double Crochet

Now you're ready to go on to a more complex stitch. To begin your first row of half double crochet, make a foundation chain that has twelve chain stitches.

HALF DOUBLE CROCHET SWATCH

Double Crochet

The double crochet has one more step to do in order to complete the stitch than a half double crochet—and that's how the half double crochet got its name. To begin your first row of double crochet, make a foundation chain that has thirteen chain stitches.

HALF DOUBLE CROCHET

1 Hold the yarn and the crochet hook as before, but for this stitch hold the foundation chain at the 4th chain stitch from the hook. Yarn over the hook from the back to the front. Insert the hook under both the front and back loops of the 3rd chain stitch from the hook. Yarn over the front of the hook and then catch the yarn with the hook. Now draw the hook through the two chain stitch loops. You now have three loops on the hook.

2 Yarn over the hook from the back to the front. Draw the hook through all three loops on the hook.

3 You have now completed one half double crochet stitch. Continue to repeat Steps 1 and 2 nine more times. You now have ten half double crochet stitches completed across the row. To proceed to the next row, make two chain stitches for the turning chain, then turn. Remember that two chain stitches equal the height of the half double crochet. To begin the next row, insert the hook under both the front and back loops of the first stitch (skipping the turning chain stitches). Continue to repeat the steps until you have completed ten rows of half double crochet. Fasten off.

DOUBLE CROCHET

1 Hold the yarn and the crochet hook as before, but for this stitch hold the foundation chain at the 5th chain stitch from the hook. Yarn over the hook from the back to the front. Insert the hook under both the front and back loops of the 4th chain stitch from the hook.

2 Yarn over the front of the hook and catch the yarn. Now draw the hook through the two chain stitch loops. You now have three loops on the hook.

3 Yarn over the hook from the back to the front. Draw the hook through the first two loops on the hook. You now have two loops remaining on the hook. Yarn over the hook from the back to the front. Draw the hook through both the loops on the hook.

4 You have now completed one double crochet stitch. Continue to repeat Steps 1–3 nine more times. You now have ten double crochet stitches completed across the row. To proceed to the next row, make three chain stitches, then turn. Remember that three chain stitches equal the height of the double crochet. Continue to repeat the steps until you have completed ten rows of double crochet. Fasten off.

DOUBLE CROCHET SWATCH

Treble Crochet

The treble crochet has one more step to do in order to complete the stitch than a double crochet. Now that you have three crochet stitches under your belt, it's time to follow slightly abbreviated directions to begin to prepare you for reading project directions. To begin your first row of treble crochet, make a foundation chain that has fourteen chain stitches.

1 Hold the foundation chain at the 6th chain stitch from the hook. Yarn over the hook two times. Insert the hook under the front and back loops of the 5th chain stitch from the hook. Yarn over and draw the hook through. You now have four loops on the hook.

2 Yarn over the hook and draw through the first two loops on the hook. You now have three loops on the hook. Yarn over the hook and draw through the next two loops on the hook. You now have two loops on the hook. Yarn over and draw through both the loops on the hook.

3 You have now completed one treble crochet. Continue to repeat Steps 1 and 2 nine more times. You now have ten treble crochet stitches completed across the row. To proceed to the next row, make four chain stitches and turn. The four chain stitches equal the height of the treble crochet. Continue to repeat the steps until you have completed ten rows. Fasten off.

Slip Stitch

The slip stitch is an odd little stitch that's shorter than a single crochet and is more utilitarian than decorative. It's used for anchoring chain stitches, shaping pieces, making drawstring cords, joining circles (called rounds) when crocheting in the round, securing seams together, finishing edges, and more. Although it is used in some pattern stitches, it is never worked in multiple rows all on its own. To practice making slip stitches, make a foundation chain that has eleven chain stitches.

1 Insert the hook under both loops of the 2nd chain from the hook. Yarn over the hook and draw through the chain stitch and then the loop on the hook in one movement. One slip stitch completed.

2 Continue to work one slip stitch in each remaining chain across. See what a nice drawstring or tie a single row of slip stitches makes.

Tip

It's almost impossible not to get interrupted when making a chain and counting chain stitches. To prevent making an error, write down the number of chain stitches you have to make on a sheet of paper. Chain-stitch in increments of ten, making a check mark on the paper for each ten chain stitches. Continue in this manner until you have reached the number required.

Loop-De-Loop

Front Loops and Back Loops

You can create new pattern stitches using the same basic stitches you've already learned by simply changing what loops you crochet into. As you explore more advanced pattern stitches, you will find some that tell you to work into a specific loop. So, give them a try and practice these versatile and important techniques.

1 Single crochet ribbing

For a ribbed pattern, crochet every row by working into the back loops only. Although you can work in any basic stitch, it looks best in single crochet (shown here) and half double crochet. This pattern stitch has a lot of stretchiness to it, making it the perfect choice for a neckband, collar, or cuff.

SIDE LINES

2 Half double crochet worked in front loops and back loops

To make a pattern stitch with subtle horizontal lines, alternate working into the back loops of one row, then into the front loops of the following row. Half double crochet is shown here, but you can use this technique for any pattern stitch with equally nice results.

EASY TEXTURE

3 Half double crochet worked in front loops and back loops across row

Create a rich crocheted fabric when you alternate working into the front loop, then the back loop across the same row. This pattern stitch looks best when worked in either single crochet or half double crochet (shown here).

Chain Links

Learning how to combine chain stitches with skipping stitches to create spaces (or holes) is your next step to creating fashion details like buttonholes and drawstrings, and the wonderful array of pattern stitches that we are sure you'll want to tackle. Here are two exercises for you to practice and get comfortable with the techniques.

Easy Eyelets

Eyelets are holes that are made by chaining, then skipping the same amount of stitches that were chained. The evenly spaced holes can be used for weaving in a drawstring or ribbon, or fastening buttons, or they can stand on their own as pretty peekaboo pattern stitches. Making them is easy, but keeping the length of the chain stitch the same width as the single crochet stitch can be a little tricky, so practicing is highly recommended.

EASY EYELETS

1 For your practice swatch, chain eighteen. Work one single crochet in the 2nd chain from the hook, then work one single crochet in each of the remaining sixteen chains—seventeen single crochet stitches. Chain one and turn. Work one single crochet in the first stitch, *chain one, skip the next stitch, then work one single crochet in the next stitch. Repeat from the * to the end of the row. Chain one and turn.

2 Work one single crochet in the first stitch, *work one single crochet in the next chain-one space, then work one single crochet in the next stitch. Repeat from the * to the end of the row. Chain one and turn. Continue to alternate rows as established until you feel comfortable with the technique and your chain stitches/spaces and single crochet stitches are all uniform in size.

Make It Mesh

Mesh patterns are like eyelet patterns, only the holes are bigger! Here you will learn to do a simple double crochet pattern with chain-two spaces. Once you grasp the concept of chaining and turning (what the numbers mean here) and where to work the last stitch of the rows, you will have the skill to undertake other openwork patterns. You will also get a leg up on doing other methods of crocheting, like working in the round.

1 For your practice swatch, chain twenty-three. Work one double crochet in the 8th chain from the hook. (Note: three of the seven chains that were skipped count as one double crochet stitch. Two chains are for the first chain-two and the other two chains equal two skipped chains.) Continue as follows: *Chain two, skip the next two chains, work one double crochet in the next chain. Repeat from the * four more times. Chain five and turn. (Note: three of the five chains count as one double crochet stitch and two chains are for the first chain-two.)

2 Skip the first stitch, *work one double crochet in the next stitch, chain two. Repeat from the * four more times. Here's where you'll see how these turning chains form a stitch and spaces. To end the row, skip the next two chains of the seven skipped chains of the row below. Work the last double crochet stitch in the 3rd chain. See how the five remaining chains (one double crochet and two skipped chains) form a corner that looks just like the opposite corner. However, a typical pattern stitch would not tell where to work the last stitch as just described. It would state: Double crochet in the 5th chain of the chain-seven. To continue, chain five and turn. (Note: Three of the five chains count as one double crochet stitch and two chains are for the first chain-two.)

3 Skip the first stitch, *work one double crochet in the next stitch, chain two. Repeat from the * four more times. Skip the next two chains of the five turning chains of the row below. Work the last double crochet stitch in the 3rd chain (or, double crochet in the 3rd chain of the chain-five). To continue, chain five and turn. To continue, repeat from the beginning of this step until you feel comfortable with the technique.

Give and Take

Learning how to increase and decrease gives you the key that unlocks the door to all sorts of wonderful pattern stitches and shaping of garment pieces. Although your first projects should be straight and narrow scarves—so you can practice chaining and turning, and making stitches uniform in size—you'll soon have the itch to advance to something a little more challenging. When you've mastered increasing and decreasing you'll have the know-how to flex your creative muscles!

Increasing in the Row

This increase is nothing more than working two (or sometimes more) stitches into one stitch. When a direction states "increase one stitch," this is the increase you'll want to use. Let's say you are making a sleeve and need to increase one stitch at each side edge. Simply work two stitches in the first stitch and two stitches in the last stitch—one stitch increased each side.

1 Use this increase when you need to increase two or more stitches at the beginning of a row. Make as many chain stitches as stitches needed to be increased, then chain for the height of the stitch you are working in. Here, three stitches are going to be increased at the beginning of a single crochet row, so chain three for the increase and chain one for the height of the single crochet stitch—four chain stitches in total.

2 Work one single crochet in the 2nd chain from the hook, then work one single crochet in each of the next two chain stitches—three single crochet stitches made. Continue to work across the rest of the row.

1 Use this increase when you need to increase two or more stitches at the end of a row. Here, the example is worked in single crochet, but you can do it in any basic stitch. To make the first increase stitch, insert the hook under the left vertical strand of the last single crochet stitch. Yarn over and draw up a loop. Yarn over and draw through both loops on the hook to complete the new single crochet stitch.

2 To make the next and all following increase stitches, insert the hook under the left vertical strand of the last single crochet stitch made. Yarn over and draw up a loop. Yarn over and draw through both loops on the hook to complete the new single crochet stitch.

1 Insert the hook into the next stitch and draw up a loop. Insert the hook into the following stitch and draw up a loop.

2 Yarn over and draw through all three loops on the hook. One single crochet stitch decreased.

Decreasing One Stitch in the Row

This technique is used to decrease one stitch over the course of two stitches. The whole idea is to work each stitch to within the last step to complete it, leaving the last loop (or loops) on the hook. You will then yarn over and draw through all the loops on the hook to combine two stitches into one.

1 Yarn over. Insert the hook into the next stitch and draw up a loop. Yarn over, insert the hook into the following stitch, and draw up a loop.

2 Yarn over and draw through all five loops on the hook. One half double crochet stitch decreased.

1 Yarn over. Insert the hook into the next stitch and draw up a loop. Yarn over and draw through two loops on the hook. Yarn over, insert the hook into the following stitch, and draw up a loop. Yarn over and draw through two loops on the hook.

2 Yarn over and draw through all three loops on the hook. One double crochet stitch decreased.

Decreasing Two or More Stitches in the Row

The same method used to decrease one stitch can be used to decrease two or more stitches. Simply work each stitch to within the last step to completion, leaving the last loop (or loops) on the hook, then yarn over and draw through all the loops on the hook.

Decreasing at the Beginning of a Row

Use this decrease when you need to decrease two or more stitches at the beginning of a row. When you have completed the last row before the decrease, do not chain; just turn the work. Work one slip stitch in each stitch that is to be decreased, here four stitches. To continue, chain for the height of the stitch you are working in (one chain for single crochet), then continue to work across the row.

Decreasing at the End of a Row

Use this decrease when you need to decrease two or more stitches at the end of a row. Simply

1 *Yarn over the hook twice. Insert the hook into the next stitch and draw up a loop. Yarn over and draw through two loops on the hook, then yarn over again and draw through two loops on the hook*. Repeat from * to * in the following stitch.

2 Yarn over and draw through all three loops on the hook. One treble crochet stitch decreased.

Four slip stitches worked at the beginning of row

Four unworked slip stitches at the end of the row

work across the row to within the last amount of stitches that need to be decreased; here, four stitches. Leaving these last stitches unworked, chain and turn to work the next row.

Going in Circles

Knowing how to crochet in the round opens up a whole other world of possibilities. Hats, booties, bags, trims, and granny squares are just some of the wonderful things you will be able to make. There are two basic methods to learn: working in a spiral and working in rounds that are joined. Knowing how to do these two techniques will prepare you for the variations that you are sure to encounter as you peruse pattern directions.

Making a Ring

No matter which method you use or whether you are making a hat from the top of the crown down or making a cuff from the bottom up, you need to start with a ring to form the foundation for your first round of stitches. The only difference between a hat and a cuff is how many chain stitches you begin with.

1 To make a practice ring, chain six. Insert the hook through both loops of the first chain stitch made. Yarn over and draw through the chain stitch and the loop on the hook in one movement.

2 You have now joined the chain with a slip stitch and formed a ring.

1 Chain five. Join the chain with a slip stitch, forming a ring. Work ten single crochets in the ring. Fasten a safety pin in the last stitch made to indicate the end of the round.

2 Work two single crochets in each of the first nine stitches. Unfasten the safety pin from the last stitch. Work two single crochets in the last

stitch. Refasten the safety pin in the last stitch made—you now have twenty stitches. To practice one more round, *work one single crochet in the next stitch, then work two single crochets in the following stitch. Repeat from the * to the end of the round, unfastening, then refastening the safety pin in the last stitch—you now have thirty stitches.

Working in a Spiral

A spiral is worked around and around without interruption. This method is usually done in single or half double crochet so there won't be a big difference in height between the beginning and the end of a round. The only tricky part is to count the stitches accurately and to keep track of the increases from one round to the next. So get a small safety pin, to be used as a stitch marker, and a pad and pencil to make notes before you begin.

Working Joined Rounds

This method can be used for any height stitch, because the beginning and end of each round are equal in height. This is accomplished by beginning each round with a chain of stitches that equal the height of the stitch being used. To end each round, a slip stitch is made in the first stitch to join the round, or in other words, complete the circle. Although this method of concentric circles is more advanced than working in a spiral, it is easier to keep track of the number of stitches because you can easily see where the round begins and ends. However, you should still keep track of the increases using a pad and pencil.

1 Chain five. Join the chain with a slip stitch forming a ring. Chain three (equals the height of a double crochet stitch). Work twelve double crochets in the ring, then join the round with a slip stitch in the top two loops of the first stitch

2 For the second round, chain three. Work two double crochet in each of the twelve stitches. Join the round with a slip stitch in the first stitch—you now have twenty-four stitches. To practice one more round, chain three, *work one double crochet in the next stitch, then work two double crochet in the following stitch. Repeat from the * to the end of the round. Join the round with a slip stitch in the first stitch—you now have thirty-six stitches.

A Few Words About Increasing

How increases are distributed around depends on three main factors: what stitch is being used, the weight of the yarn, and what shape is to be achieved. There are no hard and fast rules, but generally the taller the stitch the more stitches will be worked in the first round and all rounds thereafter, as opposed to a shorter stitch. A thinner yarn requires more stitches in the first round than a thicker yarn. To keep the work flat or to create a conical shape, there might be some rounds that have no increases at all. So expect the unexpected and just go with the flow!

Tip

To save time weaving in ends, crochet over the foundation chain tail as you work the first round of stitches into the ring.

Tied and True

Joining Yarn

So you're cruising along doing about 120 sph (stitches per hour) when you have to come to a grinding halt because you've finished the first ball of yarn! Don't fret—it's easy to get going again by joining a new ball of yarn.

Whenever you can, join the new yarn at the end of a row. This is especially important when you are crocheting an openwork or lacy pattern stitch where you have no place to weave in the yarn ends invisibly. Joining at the side might mean you'll have to cut off some of the yarn from the previous ball, but you can always use it for sewing, adding a fringe, or making a tassel. If the pattern stitch is not openwork and you find you just have to join midrow, carefully check the tension of the affected stitches to make sure they are neither too tight nor too loose.

1 To join a new ball yarn at the side edge, tie it loosely around the old yarn, leaving at least a 6"/15cm tail. Untie the knot later and weave the ends into the seam (see page 13 for how to weave in ends).

2 Before joining the new yarn midrow, complete the last stitch that you were working on. Tie the old and new ends together loosely close to the last stitch; yarn tails should be at least 6"/15cm long. Later, untie the knot and weave the ends under the stitches (see page 13 for how to weave in ends midrow).

Stripe it Right

Joining New Yarn Color

Stripes are the easiest way to create a multicolor garment, even for the beginner. But changing from one color to the next is not just a matter of tying ends together at the end of the row. The color change is actually made when you are working the last stitch of the row before, so when you chain and turn, the side edge of the next row will be entirely in the new color. How this is done varies slightly from single, half double, double, and treble crochet, but the end result will all be the same.

1 If you are working in single crochet, work across the row to within the last stitch. Insert the hook into the last stitch and draw up a loop. Working 6"/15cm from the end of the new color, draw the new color through both loops on the hook to complete the single crochet stitch.

2 Chain one and turn. Cut the old yarn leaving a 6"/15cm tail. Loosely tie the two tails together, close to the side edge, so stitches don't unravel. Later, untie the knot and weave in the ends (see bottom of page for how to weave in ends).

For Half Double Crochet

Work across the row to within the last stitch. Yarn over, insert the hook into the last stitch, and draw up a loop. Working 6"/15cm from the end of the new color, draw the new color through all three loops on the hook to complete the half double crochet stitch. Chain two and turn, then join yarns following Step 2.

For Double Crochet

Work across the row to within the last stitch. Yarn over, insert the hook into the last stitch, and draw up a loop. Yarn over and draw through two loops on the hook. Working 6"/15cm from the end of the new color, draw the new color through the last two loops on the hook to complete the double crochet stitch. Chain three and turn, then join yarns following Step 2.

For Treble Crochet

Work across the row to within the last stitch. Yarn over the hook twice, then insert the hook into the last stitch and draw up a loop. Yarn over and draw through two loops on the hook. Yarn over again and draw through two loops on the hook. Working 6"/15cm from the end of the new color, draw the new color through the last two loops on the hook to complete the treble crochet stitch. Chain four and turn, then join yarns following Step 2.

Seek and Hide

Weaving in Ends

Each time you finish a ball of yarn and join a new one or change colors for a stripe pattern, you'll find yourself with lots of loose ends. Weaving in these yarn ends is an important part of the finishing process, so it must be done properly in order to get the best end result. To do this, carefully untie the knot made when joining the new yarn. Thread one of the loose strands into a yarn needle (see "Accessorize!" on page 23) and insert the needle down through the side edge for approximately 1½"/4cm. Snip off the excess end, making sure not to cut into the crocheted fabric. To secure the second strand, thread the yarn needle with the end and weave it up the edge in the opposite direction. If you are dealing with ends from changing colors for a stripe, weave in each end along the edge of the same color.

If you have changed yarns in the middle of a row, first make sure the knot is on the wrong side of the fabric. If it isn't, push it through to the wrong side. Carefully untie the knot. Thread one loose end into a yarn needle. Weave the needle horizontally to the right for about three stitches. Before you pull the needle through, turn the work over to the right side to make sure you cannot see the needle; reweave the needle if necessary. Pull the needle through, taking care not to change the size or shape of the affected stitches. To secure, take one small backstitch, then continue to weave the needle through approximately three more stitches. Pull on the end to embed the backstitch into the fabric, flatten the fabric if it has puckered, then snip off the excess yarn end. Repeat with the remaining loose end, but weave it horizontally to the left.

Tip

Don't throw away even the smallest snippet of yarn. When your project is completed, put the scraps outside for birds to use as nesting material. Just leave them in the middle of your lawn or a similar spot, and they'll fly right in and take them away.

Building on the Basics

Learning about crochet is like immersing yourself in a foreign culture where another language is spoken and written, and where there are unfamiliar rules and customs. It can be a little intimidating and a tad frustrating at times, but the payoff is big and totally worthwhile. So continue to follow along as we explain what you'll need to know before you make your very first project!

Gauge

The longest journey begins with the first step, and knowing the importance of gauge is your first step to crocheting a garment that comes out the correct size. Every pattern direction will have a recommended gauge, plus finished measurements. The gauge is how many stitches and rows you should get over a span of inches/centimeters (usually a 4"/10cm square) when you work in the specified pattern stitch, using the yarn and crochet hook size called for in the materials list. The amount of stitches to the inch/centimeter (or gauge) dictates how many stitches will be crocheted to achieve the finished measurements.

Tip

Don't unravel the gauge swatch; instead, save it for any repairs the garment might need during its lifetime. Wash the swatch along with the garment so the yarns will always match perfectly.

The second step is making a gauge swatch, which enables you to make sure you get the recommended gauge before you begin your project. While the gauge is based on a 4"/10cm square, you should make a swatch that's at least a 5"/12.5cm square to be better able to measure accurately. Gather up the same yarn and crochet hook size that is called for in the directions. Crochet enough chain stitches for a 5"/12.5cm-wide swatch, then work in the pattern stitch specified in the directions for 5"/12.5cm. Do not fasten off. Place the swatch on a hard, flat surface. For stitches across, place a ruler, tape measure, or stitch gauge horizontally on the swatch. Position the 1"/2.5cm mark even with a whole stitch, then working toward the right, count 4"/10cm worth of stitches (don't forget fractions of stitches). If you have more stitches to the inch/centimeter than is recommended, remake the swatch using a hook that's one size larger. If you have fewer stitches than is stated, try again with a smaller hook.

GAUGE

If you think that making a gauge swatch is unnecessary, think again! Each one of these single crochet gauge swatches was made using the same yarn and have the exact same amount of stitches and rows. The swatch on the left was made using a hook that was only one size smaller than the swatch on the right. Just imagine how this would impact the overall size of a sweater. We hope this convinces you not to take shortcuts!

MEASURING GAUGE

You can measure your gauge swatch using a ruler, as the first two photos show. Or you can use a stitch gauge in the center of your swatch and count the stitches and rows inside the 2"/5cm right-angle opening (as shown in the third photo).

Once you have achieved the recommended gauge, it's time to begin your project! But you'll still want to recheck your gauge once you have crocheted about 5"/12.5cm of work. Just as before, place the piece on a flat surface and measure the total width to see if it matches the width stated in the finished measurements. If it does, you're good to go, but if it doesn't you'll have to change your hook size. "But why isn't it the right size?" you might ask. This is because sometimes you might crochet looser or tighter (this is called the tension) when you work across a larger piece of fabric. If you find that you have to change the hook size to get the right gauge, you'll have to unravel all the rows and start again using one size larger hook (if it's too small) or one size smaller hook (if it's too large). This might

Tip

Don't be influenced by other crocheters who say they never bother making a gauge swatch. Just keep in mind that professional crochet designers—those creative artists who design the projects that you will be making and wearing—have to make a gauge swatch before they are able to calculate all numbers of stitches and rows needed to form a garment. In order for you to get the same results as the picture of the sweater that you fell in love with, you'll have to match their gauge, stitch for stitch and row for row.

seem heartbreaking and discouraging, but just imagine how you'd feel when after spending hours to complete the piece you discover that the size is all wrong.

Abbreviations and Terms

The first time you look at the directions for a crochet pattern stitch or directions for a project, you may think it's written in a foreign language. But on second glance you'll begin to see recognizable words emerging, no matter how much they were shortened. But why condense words and phrases? Well, consider if everything were written out in whole words and sentences; directions that would normally fit on one page now become a whole book! It's actually easier to learn the language of crochet than to wade through pages and pages of directions. At right is a list of abbreviations and terms that you'll encounter as you continue to explore crochet. Keep this page bookmarked, so you can refer to it as needed.

Understanding Schematics

Although these little drawings look like sewing patterns for a fashion doll, they are actually drawn-to-scale outlines of what each piece of a sweater should look like and measure after it has been crocheted. Called schematics, they are essential to your decision-making and the ultimate success of a project. When you are considering making a sweater, look at the schematics first. Simple outlines, such as those shown here, usually mean it's a beginner-level project because there is no shaping on the front and back and the sleeve is pretty straightforward. Generally the more shaping involved—like a tapered waist, V-neck, and slanted shoulders—the more advanced the project. Also consider the style; maybe you don't like how dropped shoulders look on you.

Each main piece of the sweater will be shown as a separate schematic; pieces like pockets are not shown unless they are shaped. Note here that the front and the back are shown as one, or more accurately, one is superimposed on the other. This is usually the case, except when the front and back are drastically different in size and shape. For a cardigan, only one front will be represented, except, of course, when the left front is different than the right.

So what are all these numbers? All schematics will have the same general information as shown. For the front and back: bottom width/bust measurement, length to armhole, armhole depth, shoulder width, neck width, and total length from bottom edge to top. For the sleeve: cuff width, total length from bottom edge

to top edge, and width of top edge. Keep in mind that if there is other shaping, like a V-neck, the measurements for the depth (where you begin and end) will be shown as well. When reading the numbers, the smallest size is listed first, before the parentheses, and each larger size will be inside the parentheses in sequential order.

Tip

To avoid confusion, and perhaps making a mistake, use a yellow marker to highlight the measurements on the schematics that pertain to the size you are making.

approx: approximately
beg: begin, beginning
[ ]: Repeat the directions inside the brackets as many times as indicated.
ch: chain, chains
cont: continue, continuing
CC: contrasting color
dec: decrease, decreasing
dc: double crochet (UK: tr—treble)
hdc: half double crochet (UK: htr—half treble)
inc: increase, increasing
lp/lps: loop/loops
MC: main color
mm: millimeter, millimeters
oz/g: ounces/grams. This usually refers to the amount of yarn in a single skein, ball, or hank of yarn.
( ): Work the directions contained inside the parentheses into the stitch indicated. See "Small (Medium, Large)," at right, for the other uses of parentheses.
pat/pats: pattern, patterns

rem: remain, remains, or remaining
rep: repeat, repeating
rep from *: Repeat the directions following the asterisk as many times as indicated. If the directions say "rep from * to end," continue to repeat the directions after the asterisk to the end of the row.
rev sc: reverse single crochet
reverse shaping: A term used for garments such as cardigans, where shaping for the right and left fronts is identical but reversed. For example, neck edge stitches that were decreased at the beginning of the row for the first piece will be decreased at the end of the row on the second piece. In general, follow the directions for the first piece, making sure to mirror the decreases (and/or increases) on each side.
RS: right side, right sides
rnd/rnds: round/rounds
sc: single crochet (UK: dc—double crochet)

sk: skip, skipping
sl: slip, slipping
sl st: slip stitch (UK: sc—single crochet)
Small (Medium, Large): The most common method of displaying changes in a pattern for different sizes. In general, stitch counts, measurements, etc., for the smallest size come first, followed by the larger sizes in parentheses. If there is only one number given, it applies to all of the sizes.
sp/sps: space/spaces
st/sts: stitch/stitches
t-ch: turning chain
tog: together
tr: treble crochet (UK: dtr—double treble)
work even: Continue in the established pattern without working any increases or decreases.
WS: wrong side, wrong sides
yd/m: yard(s)/meter(s)
yo: yarn over

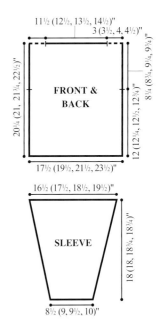

Measuring Up

Blocking

Although the word "blocking" sounds ominous, like something that should be avoided, it's actually one of the most important steps to successfully completing your garment. In essence, blocking is a method of shaping and molding your crocheted pieces to match the measurements and shapes on the schematics. Blocking will also remove wrinkles and creases that might occur if the pieces have been folded.

Keep in mind that blocking is only to shape and not to correct mistakes by making a piece wider or longer so it matches another piece. Unlike most grunt work, the payoff to a successfully blocked garment is huge. With some time and effort the end result will be a beautiful sweater that looks lovingly handmade rather than a home-made mess.

There are two main categories of blocking: wet and steam. To know which one to use with the yarn that was used for your project, refer to the ball band for the fiber content and to the Pressing Guide (on this page). To get started, gather up all the supplies you'll need, including the schematics or the measurements from the pattern. The schematics and measurements will serve as a blueprint for you to follow, so you'll know exactly what size and shape the pieces should be stretched and molded into.

Wet Blocking

There are two ways to wet block your crocheted pieces. Both techniques work equally well, so choose the one that appeals to you most. The first is to immerse the pieces in cool water, then squeeze out the water, taking care not to wring or twist them. Working one at a time, place the piece on a flat, covered, padded surface (or a blocking board), then stretch and mold the piece into the same size and shape shown on the schematic. Referring to "Pinning and Blocking," pin the key edges to hold the piece in shape until it is totally dry. Depending on the room temperature and humidity, drying time can be in excess of twenty-four hours, so just be patient.

The second method is to pin the pieces first (following the schematics), then wet them down using a spray bottle filled with cool water. Again, leave them be until they are dry. And no cheating! If you unpin pieces that are even slightly damp, they will lose the blocked shape and you will have to start all over again!

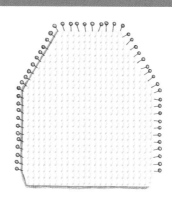 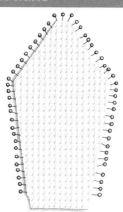

1 Pin the key areas as shown, omitting the bottom edge. For perfectly straight edges, make sure to space the pins evenly.

2 Following the schematic, use a tape measure to make sure you pin the piece evenly to the padded surface.

All fibers react differently to heat, so it's a good idea to know what to expect before you press or steam them (or even if you should). Many yarns are a combination of fibers, so you should choose a method that is compatible with all the contents. Read the ball band to see what fiber has the highest percentage, then go with the recommended method for that fiber first. Test the method on your gauge swatch to see the results and determine if you have to make any adjustments before committing the technique to your garment pieces.

Angora	Wet block by spraying.
Cotton	Wet block or warm/hot steam press.
Linen	Wet block or warm/hot steam press.
Lurex	Do not block.
Mohair	Wet block by spraying.
Novelties	Do not block, unless there are specific blocking directions.
Synthetics	Carefully follow instructions on ball band—usually wet block by spraying; do not press.
Wool and all wool-like fibers (alpaca, camel hair, cashmere)	Wet block by spraying or warm steam press.
Wool blends	Wet block by spraying; do not press unless pretested first.

Steam Blocking

To steam block, first pin the pieces on a flat surface following the measurements on the schematics. Set your steam iron on the lowest setting that will still produce steam, or use a handheld steamer. Once you have a good steam going, hold the iron or steamer close to the fabric, then work in a circular motion over the entire piece until every inch is evenly dampened.

DO NOT touch the iron to the fabric! If you find that you must lightly press the piece, cover it with a colorfast towel or a pressing cloth to protect the fabric from the hot metal plate. Drying after steaming takes a lot less time than wet blocking, but you still must allow the pieces to dry thoroughly before unpinning.

I Flat, covered, padded surface large enough to hold one piece of crochet and thick enough to insert and hold pins (such as a carpet or mattress covered with plastic and a towel). Or you might want to invest in a blocking board, which is easier to use and more convenient (although a little pricey).

2 Rustproof T-pins or glass-headed pins. Do not use pins with plastic heads. They will melt when they come in contact with heat.

3 Tape measure

4 Schematic for the sweater you are blocking

5 Colorfast towels

6 Spray bottle with cool water or a sinkful of cool water

7 Steam iron or handheld steamer

8 Pressing cloth

Construction Zone

Order of Assembling

When you've finished crocheting the pieces for a sweater, it's time to assemble them. (Before you thread your yarn needle, you should block the pieces first to get the most professional-looking results; see page 16.) There is a certain order to putting pieces together, and for good reason. Not to follow the order is like putting the cart before the horse. All sweater patterns have finishing directions at the end. The finishing directions will state what and when to sew and how to complete unfinished edges, like a neckline. As an example, here's what you should expect to find for a crewneck pullover that has dropped-shoulder sleeves: First, sew the shoulder seams. Second, finish the neck edge (with a neckband, trim, etc.). Third, sew the sleeves to the body of the sweater. And fourth, sew the side and sleeve seams. This is done in one continuous seam, from the end of the sleeve to the underarm and then down the body of the sweater to the bottom edge.

Marking for Armholes

The simplest sweater to make is one with dropped shoulders. Although the top edges of the sleeves are straight and the side edges of the body are straight, it can be a little tricky to sew the sleeves evenly to the body. First, let's get a handle on how to mark for the beginning of the armholes, then we'll discuss how to sew the sleeves evenly in place.

Where or how to mark for the armholes depends on the way a sweater direction is written. You will encounter two ways, and both are acceptable. The first way is when you have crocheted the stated amount of inches to the underarms. The directions will say: "Mark beginning and end of last row for beginning of armholes." To mark, simply fasten one safety pin to the beginning of the last row and one to the end of the last row. Continue to work following the directions, until you have reached the armhole measurement stated in the directions. Before you join the sleeves, join the shoulders (referring to the finishing directions).

The second way is when the directions have you mark for the armholes after the shoulders are joined. To mark, lay the sweater out flat on a flat surface. Measure down from the center of the shoulder seam along the side edge of the back (or front) to the stated amount of inches (take care not to stretch the fabric!), then fasten a safety pin. Repeat along the front (or back) side edge, then mark for the armholes along the opposite front and back side edges. Just to make sure that all things are equal, also measure from the safety-pin marks down to the bottom edges. Make any adjustments necessary.

Now that you know how to mark for the armholes, here's how to center the sleeves in the armholes. Using a tape measure, measure and mark (using a straight pin) the center of the top edges of the sleeves. Place each sleeve along the armhole edge between the armhole markers and so the straight-pin mark is centered in the center of the shoulder seam. Join each sleeve following the seaming directions (page 18). Don't forget to remove all the pins!

Measuring Length

Whenever you have two pieces that are to be joined together, they must be the same length. For a cardigan, both fronts and back should be the exact same length. Mis-matched seams will give you a lopsided sweater that will not only fit poorly but look silly. The same goes for sleeves. Each should be equal in length so that when you wear the sweater, each cuff will fall at the same point on both wrists. There are two ways to tackle the issue of length. The first is to measure precisely using a tape measure. Lay the piece on a flat surface and measure the length without stretching the piece in either direction. Pulling on the fabric to make it meet a measurement is only a temporary solution. Yarn has a memory and will spring back to its original shape once tension has been released.

The second way to ensure equal lengths is to count rows. This is the most reliable method. You can either opt for a row counter or go for the old paper and pencil. Mark or check off the row as you are about to crochet it, so you'll always know where you are and have an accurate count. But just in case a row or two is missed, recount the rows just to be absolutely sure of the count before you fasten off the last stitch.

Seams Easy

Once you've fastened off the last stitch of all your garment pieces, it's time to assemble them into something you can wear. There are a few ways to join crochet pieces together, and each version serves a different purpose. Some use a yarn needle and are woven or sewn together and some use a crochet hook and are crocheted together. In most instances you will use the same yarn that was used for your project. For the most part you want to join edges together neatly without creating bulky seams. However, sometimes you need a very sturdy seam for a garment that will get a lot of wear, so a little bulk is a small price to pay for longevity.

Some garments may require a more sturdy or even a thinner yarn for seaming. This may allow for better fit. Experiment with different types of yarn to determine the most suitable yarn for seaming. For example: when crocheting with a thin mohair yarn you may choose to seam with a smooth wool yarn of similar weight in a matching color. You can even choose an embroidery floss thread to seam with, as it is thin and comes in a wide array of colors.

1 This method gives you an invisible seam with no bulk. Work on a flat surface. With the right sides of both pieces facing you, and the two edges adjoined, secure with safety pins every 2"/5cm. Thread a yarn needle with the tail from the foundation chain. To secure the edges together before weaving, insert the needle from back to front into the corner stitch of the piece without the tail. Making a figure eight with the yarn, insert the needle, from back to front, into the stitch with the tail. Tighten to close up the gap.

2 To begin weaving the seam, insert the needle through the first stitch on the left edge and then through the first stitch on the right edge. Insert the needle through the next stitch on the left edge and then through the next stitch on the right edge. Continue to alternate weaving from edge to edge in this manner, carefully matching stitches (or rows) and drawing the yarn only tight enough to keep the edges together.

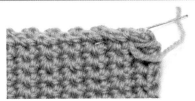 

1 The backstitch is used when you need a seam that's extra strong and bulk is not an issue. Place the pieces together so the right sides are facing, then pin every 2"/5cm. Thread the tail from the foundation chain into the yarn needle. Working from back to front, secure the beginning of the seam by taking the needle twice around the bottom edges. Working from back to front again, insert the needle so it exits about ¼"/5mm from the last stitch, as shown.

2 Insert the needle into the same hole as the last stitch, then back up approximately ¼"/5mm in front of the last stitch. Draw the yarn through, then tighten only enough to keep the edges together. Continue to work in this manner, taking care to keep the stitches straight and the same length.

The whipstitch is used for joining squares for an afghan together, like grannies, as well as other short, straight edges. Thread the tail from the foundation chain in a yarn needle. Place the pieces together so the wrong-side sides are facing, edges are even, and stitches line up. Insert the needle into the back loop of the piece in front and into the front loop of the adjacent stitch of the piece in back. Continue to work in this manner, drawing the yarn only tight enough to keep the edges together.

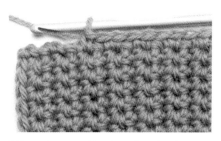

1 Use this method for decorative exterior seams. Working from the ball of yarn, make a slip knot 6"/15cm from the yarn end. Place the slip knot on the hook. To work across top edges, place the pieces together so wrong sides are facing. Working from front to back, insert the crochet hook through both loops of each piece and draw through a loop. Yarn over and draw through both loops on the hook. Continue to work one single crochet in each pair of adjacent loops across.

2 To work across side edges, place the pieces together so wrong sides are facing. Working through both thicknesses, work single crochet stitches directly into matching stitches at the side edge, making sure to space them evenly and at the same depth so that all single crochet stitches are the same size.

Use this technique when you want an especially sturdy joining but don't mind the extra bulk. Place the pieces together with right sides facing and edges even; pin every 2"/5cm. Working through both thicknesses and from front to back, insert the crochet hook between the first two stitches, one stitch in from the edge. Working from the ball of yarn, catch the yarn on the wrong side (about 6"/15cm from the end) and draw through a loop. *Insert the hook between the next two stitches. Draw through a loop, then draw through the loop on the hook. Repeat from the *, keeping an even tension on the yarn so the stitches are even in size and the joining has the same stretchiness as the crocheted fabric.

Going Straight

Across a Straight Edge

Most times you'll need to either finish a raw edge; set the foundation row for a collar, button-hole band, or cuff; or add a border to an afghan square. Depending on the design and directions, this is done with the same yarn and color, the same yarn but in a contrasting color, or a totally different yarn that might not even be the same weight. So how hard is it to crochet across a straight edge? Well, unless it's done perfectly, it can look unattractive.

There are two things you need to remember when you are crocheting along an edge. The first is to make sure the right side of the fabric is facing you. Project directions will always state "with right side facing" or "from right side," but it's good for you to know this from the beginning. The second is to space the stitches evenly while making sure the fabric lies flat.

It's easy to work across the top edge (last row) using the same yarn that was used to crochet the pieces, because you simply work one stitch into each stitch across. But when you're working with a yarn that is not the same weight there are a few things you should know so you will get the best results. If you are using a thinner yarn, you'll need a smaller hook. To work evenly across, you'll be working one stitch in some stitches and two stitches in others. The places where there are two stitches should be evenly spaced so all the stitches form a uniform pattern. On the other hand, if you are using a thicker yarn, you'll need to use a larger hook. To work evenly across, you'll be working one stitch in some stitches and skipping others. The skipped stitches should likewise be evenly spaced. Spacing stitches evenly takes some practice, so you might have to rip out and start

Tip

To anchor the yarn securely when you are going to work along an edge, make a slip knot in the yarn, about 8"/20.5cm from the end, and place it on the hook. Keep the slip knot on the hook until you have made a few stitches. Carefully remove the working loop from the hook, then the slip knot; place the working loop back on the hook. Pull the free end of the slip knot to undo it. Use the 8"/20.5cm end for seaming or simply weave it in.

over a few times until you get the hang of it. Remember, the whole objective is to be flat and even. If there are too many stitches, the edge will flare out. If there are too few stitches, the edge will pull in.

When working vertically, crochet stitches directly into the stitches at the side edge. Not only should you make sure to space them evenly but go into the stitches at the same depth, so that all stitches are the same size. If the edging is being added in preparation for seaming (like afghan squares), also take care to work an equal number of edge stitches on all pieces so they will all match up perfectly.

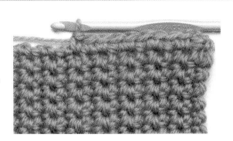

CROCHETING ACROSS THE BOTTOM EDGE

When working across the bottom edge, work each stithc between two stitches rather than working into the bottom loops of the foundation chain. (Note: Working through the bottom loops will add length, so only work through them when directions tell you to.), If you are using a yarn of a different weight, follow the same technique as described for working across the top edge.

Taking the Curves

Working Along the Neck

Crocheting along a neck edge, or any rounded edge, takes just a little more care than for a straight edge because the even distribution of stitches is crucial to the overall fit and appearance. Having too many stitches in one section will make the trim, neckband, or collar bulge or flare out, and having too few stitches will make it pucker.

When working along curved or vertical edges, follow the technique as for crocheting along a side edge (above), making sure all stitches are the same size. When working across straight or horizontal edges (center front and back neck), use the same technique as for working across a straight edge (page 19).

MARKING NECK EDGE FOR SPACING STITCHES

Stitches must be distributed evenly so a trim, neckband, or collar will not flare out or pull in. Place pins, safety pins, or yarn markers as shown, every 2"/5cm. If you know the number of stitches to be crocheted, divide this by the number of sections marked to determine how many stitches to work between each pair of markers. If no number is given in the directions, use the marked sections to ensure even spacing around the neck.

Tip

If the trim, buttonhole band, or collar is going to be crocheted using a contrasting color, you can make the transition more seamless when you work the first row in single crochet using the main yarn color.

Sew Perfect

Sewing on Trims

Sometimes neckbands, collars, and cuffs are made separately, then sewn in place. These bands are usually worked in single crochet, where each stitch is worked in the back loop to create a ribbed effect (see page 8 and at right). The bands are made a little shorter then the total length of the neck edge or sleeve edge, so they will hug the neck or wrist. To make sure they are sewn on evenly, place markers every 2"/5cm along the neck or sleeve edge. Place the same amount of markers along the edge of the band,

MARKING A TRIM FOR SEWING

The bands are made a little shorter than the total length of the neck edge or sleeve edge. After marking the neck or sleeve edge in 2"/5cm intervals, place the same amount of markers along the edge of the band, making sure to space them evenly.

making sure to space them evenly. With right sides facing, pin the band in place, matching markers on the edge with markers on the band, then sew in place.

Button Up!

Buttons and buttonholes can make or break the look of a sweater. Poorly spaced buttons and buttonholes that are too big are just two of the potential problems. As a beginner you should follow the pattern directions for the size and the amount of buttons needed and how far apart you should space them. But sometimes it's just too hard to resist putting your personal mark on your own sweater. So whether you plan to stick to the directions or want to get creative, read on.

TWO-ROW BUTTONHOLES

1 Work to the placement marker of the buttonhole (single crochet shown here). Chain three (not too loosely), skip the next three stitches, then continue to work to the end of the row or to the next marker.

2 On the next row, work to the chain-three space. Work three stitches in the space, then continue to work to the end of the row or to the next chain-three space.

Two-Row Buttonhole

The two-row buttonhole is the most common way to make a buttonhole. It's not only easy to do, using techniques you have already learned, it can be made to accommodate just about any size button. It is made by crocheting a number of chain stitches, then skipping the same amount of stitches as were chained. On the following row, the same number of stitches are crocheted into the chain-space as were chained and skipped. Keep in mind that the fewer the number of stitches chained and skipped, the smaller the buttonhole, and vice versa.

If you are going to use a button size that's different than what's called for, you must first crochet a swatch, using the same pattern stitch that's used in the directions, and experiment to see how many chain stitches you need to make and skip. To test for size, slide the button through the hole. The width of the buttonhole should be slightly smaller than the width of the button, otherwise the button will not stay buttoned.

Buttonhole Spacing

The first step to perfect spacing and matching up of buttons and buttonholes is to measure and

mark the spacing of the buttons. Pattern directions will always tell you where to place the first and last button; but then what? To get your buttons spaced as evenly as possible, start by placing markers on the buttonhole band for the first and last buttons. If there are an odd number of buttons, measure and place a third marker in the center. Measure the distance between these markers, then place evenly spaced markers for the remaining buttons. For speedier and more accurate marking, use straight pins first. They are easiest to position and reposition by even a fraction of an inch. When all your markings are completed, replace the straight pins with more secure safety pins or yarn markers.

Although the two-row buttonhole is made only one way, it will take on two different looks depending on how the buttonhole band is made. When the buttonhole band is made from the bottom up, the buttonhole will be a horizontal slit.

When the buttonhole band is crocheted directly onto the front edge of a cardigan front, for example, the buttonhole will be a vertical slit. In order for you to evenly match buttons to buttonholes you'll have to know two different methods of measuring. To make sure your buttons and horizontal buttonholes line up exactly, simply count the number of rows between the lower edge and the first marker, between the first and second markers, etcetera. Write down how many rows separate each marker, and then make your buttonholes on the corresponding rows of the buttonhole band.

Matching vertical buttonholes to buttons is a little trickier because you have to center the buttonhole on the button. The marker not only indicates the placement of the button but the center of the buttonhole. If the buttonhole is only one stitch wide, make the buttonhole at the marker. If the buttonhole is two to three stitches wide, begin the buttonhole one stitch before the marker. If the buttonhole is four to five stitches wide, begin the buttonhole two stitches before the marker. Also keep in mind that the number of stitches between the buttonholes should all be the same.

Button Loops

Button loops are worked on the right side of the crocheted fabric edge and are usually completed in one row. Typically, the row is worked in single crochet, but the loops are always made of chain stitches. If you are going to give button loops a try, experiment first to see how many chain stitches you'll need to create a loop that's big enough for your button but small enough to keep the button in place.

One-Step Button Loop

These simple loops are usually used for buttoning the shoulders of infants' and children's pullovers or the fronts of cardigans. However, when you are working with a thicker yarn, such as chunky or bulky weight, they can be used for adult sweaters as well; finer yarns make flimsy loops for adult-size garments.

Two-Step Button Loop

These very sturdy loops are perfect for fastening just about any size or shape button and add a handsome designer detail as well. Make a test swatch following our general directions (see page 14) to familiarize yourself with this technique. To make custom-sized loops, simply adjust the amount of chain stitches and skipped stitches. After you know how many stitches you must skip, you will then be able to measure and mark for their placement.

Sewing Success

For the average sweater that gets light wear, you can use the same yarn that was used to crochet the sweater for sewing on the buttons. Just be sure the yarn can go through the holes in the button. If it's too thick, use matching sewing thread instead. To increase the strength of the thread, use the thread doubled in the needle and

(see page 14)

ONE-STEP BUTTON LOOP

Work to the placement marker of the button loop (single crochet shown here). Crochet the desired number of chain stitches (not too loosely), either don't skip any stitches or skip one or two, then continue to work to the end of the row or to the next marker.

TWO-STEP BUTTON LOOP

1 Work in single crochet for about ten stitches. Chain four and turn so the wrong side is facing you. Skip two stitches, then work one slip stitch in the next stitch.

2 Chain one and turn so the right side is facing you. Work six single crochets in the loop or as many single crochet stitches needed to cover the loop. To continue, single crochet in the next stitch of the edge.

ANCHORING THE THREAD

Knotted thread can pull through crocheted fabric, so use this neat little trick to secure it in place. Insert the double-threaded needle into the fabric from front to back to front again. Now insert the needle between the threads at the knotted end, as shown, then pull the needle to take in the slack. Trim the excess thread close to the knot.

Tip

Sew one or two spare buttons onto the gauge swatch in case you need replacements. Buttons (like yarn) can change color when washed, so wash the swatch along with the garment and not only will the yarn match, the buttons will, too.

Tip

When shopping for buttons, be sure to bring the sweater directions, the picture of the sweater, and a ball or swatch of the yarn. It's important to know the correct size and number of buttons you'll need and to be able to choose the right color and style. The picture will give you a good idea how the buttons you choose will look on your finished sweater.

tie the ends together in a tight, secure knot. For metal buttons that can gnaw through yarn and regular sewing thread in no time, opt for carpet thread or even dental floss.

Buttons cause the most wear and tear on a garment, so it's a good idea to add an extra bit of security in the form of a backup button; this is especially important for jackets that get the heaviest wear. When you buy your fashion buttons, also buy the same amount of shirt buttons

in a color that matches the yarn. To attach a backup button, have the fashion button on the right side of the crocheted fabric and the shirt button behind it on the wrong side. Sew the two buttons together, going through the fabric and their corresponding holes. It's important not to sew them too tightly together. Leave a little wiggle room so it will be easy to button and unbutton, and the fabric behind the fashion button can't pucker.

Accessorize!

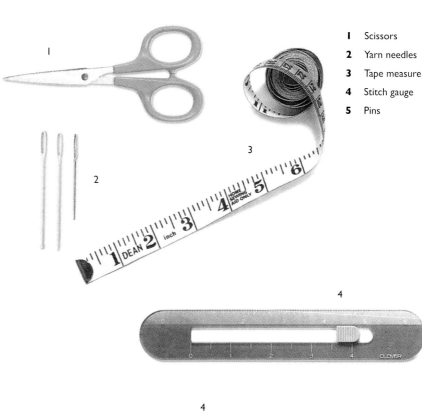

1   Scissors

2   Yarn needles

3   Tape measure

4   Stitch gauge

5   Pins

Tools of the Trade

There are some essential gadgets you'll need now and some you'll need later when you go on to more advanced projects. Many of them were designed with the knitter in mind and some are even labeled as such, but they can serve the crocheter just as well. Luckily these tools are all fairly inexpensive, so putting together a kit won't cost you much. Find something roomy to keep them in, like a zippered cosmetics bag, a lidded tin, or a plastic box that snaps shut.

Scissors

A good pair of sharp scissors is a must-have. Choose a small size with sharp points that will allow you to get close to the work when snipping off loose ends. Buy a pair that come in a case, or fashion a case yourself from felt (if you sew) or even two pieces of cardboard that are simply taped together. The case will not only protect you from getting jabbed, it will protect the tips from getting damaged.

Yarn Needles

These large-eyed, blunt-tipped needles are used for sewing seams, weaving in yarn ends, and doing embroidered embellishments. Also known as tapestry needles, they are made out of metal or plastic and come in different sizes. It's a good idea to keep a variety of sizes in your kit, so you'll always have the right one for whatever weight yarn was used to make your project.

Tape Measure

When it comes to measuring more than just a few inches, a ruler just doesn't measure up. Choose a tape measure that's made of fiberglass and has inches marked on one side and centimeters on the other. A retractable one is even better, because it won't get tangled up with your other tools. Over time and with a lot of use, a tape measure can crack, stretch, and numbers can get worn off. So you may need to consider replacing it once a year.

Stitch Gauge

This odd-looking, perforated metal rectangle is one of the most useful tools you can have in your kit. It not only measures stitch and row gauges, it measures crochet hook sizes and is a ruler as well! To measure gauge, lay your crocheted swatch on a flat surface and then line up the L-shaped window with the corner of a stitch. Count the number of stitches in the window

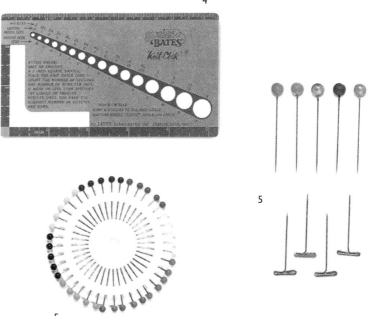

(both horizontally and vertically) to get accurate stitch and row gauges. To measure the size of an unmarked crochet hook, insert the shaft of the hook into holes of increasing size until you reach the one that allows the hook to slide through. The hole's corresponding number is your hook's size. Use the 6"/15cm ruler when you need to measure just a couple of inches/centimeters.

Pins

Trying to block finished pieces without pinning is just begging for trouble. Sleeves won't match in length and width, nor will the front and back. For blocking, you'll need lots of rustproof T-pins. The flat top of the "T" makes it easy to insert them into padding and just as easy to pull out once you're done. Because you need so many, it's best to keep them stored in a small tin or box rather than in a pin cushion.

It is just as important to pin seams together before sewing as it is pinning before blocking. If you don't pin, you run the risk of uneven edges and stripes and pattern repeats that don't match along the seam. To pin seams, you'll need straight pins with colored glass heads. They are easy to see against the crocheted fabric and easy to find and remove when you're done. Keep them in a small box or pin cushion.

Safety pins are a must-have because they can be used in a number of ways. Use them to hold together pieces that are to be sewn and to mark stitches and rows. When it's time to put away your work, slip the loop off the hook, then fasten it with a safety pin to prevent the stitches from accidentally unraveling. Always have a good variety of sizes on hand and fasten them together so they won't be so easy to lose.

Row Counters

To keep track of pattern stitch rows and to make sure that front and back pieces match up exactly, not to mention making sleeves that are exact duplicates, you'll need to count rows. But it's just impossible trying to remember what pattern stitch row you're on or where to increase and decrease with everything else that you have to think about. So put your mind at ease and put your trust in a tracking system that you can buy or make yourself.

A pegboard counter keeps track of worked rows, pattern stitch rows, and increases and decreases all at the same time. It's a very ingenious gadget that works just like an abacus. Or use this same type of system on a pad of lined paper. Simply make a separate column and label it for each item you have to

6

7

9

8

6 Stitch markers
7 Pompom maker
8 Bobbins
9 Knitting spool

keep track of. Write down the number of pattern rows and how often you have to increase or decrease. Check off each row as you are about to do it and always finish the row before you put away your project. This way you'll always know where you ended and where you should begin.

Stitch Markers

These little gadgets are absolutely necessary for indicating where to increase and decrease, where an armhole begins, marking the end of a circular row, buttonhole placement, etc. The

best stitch markers to use are good old-fashioned safety pins. While there are plastic markers that have slits that make it possible to attach them to the crocheted fabric, they can be clumsy to use and can even snag the yarn. But safety pins are a snap to handle, the sharp tips never damage the yarn, and best of all, they stay put where you fasten them. For marking that doesn't need to be moved, such as the placement for buttonholes, you can also use short lengths of contrasting yarn that can be simply tied in place.

Pompom Makers

Sure, it's easy to make a pompom without the benefit of one of these doughnut-shaped disks, but it's hard to make it look perfect, not to mention how much yarn you'll waste giving it a "haircut." You'll take all the guesswork out of making perfect pompoms, in just about every size, when you invest in a set of these disks. There are many variations of a basic pompom maker on the market, so follow the package directions that comes with the one you purchase to get the best results. (See page 28 for tutorial.)

Bobbins

Bobbins are used for projects that feature more than one color yarn. These flat pieces of plastic that hold a few yards of yarn that are a lot easier to handle than trying to wrestle with and untangle whole balls of yarn. To use, simply wind the yarn horizontally around the center of the bobbin, then slip the yarn end through the slit to anchor it in place. When it's time to use that color, slip the yarn from the slit, unwind what you need, then slip the yarn end back through the slit to "lock" it in place. Bobbins come in different sizes, so opt for the size that's right for the yarn being used: smaller bobbins for finer yarns and larger bobbins for bulkier yarns.

Knitting Spools

You might already have one of these little gizmos stuck in a drawer somewhere around your house. Along with lanyards made from plastic lacing, the knitting spool kept a kid's idle hands busy during the long days of summer. So dust it off or buy one new to make cords that you can use for drawstrings, hat ties, and more!

Notebook

Little scraps of paper can get lost in no time, but a notebook is easy to keep track of. Use it to record everything from sizes and measurements of you and whomever you want to make garments for, what projects you have completed, what projects you plan on making, and in what book and on what page a pattern stitch can be located. Staple the ball band to the page of the project you are working on, so that its important information will always be at hand. A looseleaf binder is your best bet, because you can easily add and remove pages.

Work Bag

Whether you plan to take it on the road or sit in front of the TV, you'll need a roomy tote to hold your project, yarn, and accessories. Choose one with comfortable straps and sturdy, straight sides so that the bag can stand on its own and not collapse. An inside pocket is a plus for holding supplies, but a zipper closure is a must to keep dirt out and all your items in. If all of your crocheting will be done at home, you might opt for a large lidded basket that blends in with your décor.

> ### Tip
> Always keep your work-in-progress in a fresh plastic bag, then inside your work bag or tote. Choose a bag size that's the right size for your project. Change the bag for each new project, to prevent yarn fibers from one project getting on the next.

Get Hooked

This self-striping scarf proves that style and ease are not mutually exclusive. Simple single crochet makes this the perfect project to develop smooth stitches and learn the basics with a sassy, chic result.

Gauge

16 sts and 19 rows to 4"/10cm over sc using size I/9 (5.5mm) crochet hook.
Take time to check gauge.

Scarf

Ch 24.
Row 1 Sc in 2nd ch from hook and in each ch across—23 sts. Ch 1, turn.
Row 2 Sc in each st across. Ch 1, turn.
Rep row 2 for pat st and work even until you have finished the third ball of yarn; piece should measure approx 51"/129.5cm from beg.
Fasten off. Weave in ends.

Crocheted Measurements
- Approx 5¾" x 51"/15 x 129.5cm

Materials
- 3 1¾oz/50g balls (each approx 147yd/135m) of Lion Brand Amazing (wool and acrylic) in Aurora #1518 (4)
- Size I/9 (5.5mm) crochet hook or *size to obtain gauge*

> ### Tip
> When you sit down to crochet, always make sure you have plenty of good light with no glare and no harsh shadows; never rely on only one lamp for light. To further prevent eyestrain, check with your optometrist to see if you need eyeglasses for crocheting. Even if you don't need glasses to read, you might need them for crocheting because the comfortable distance you hold a book from your eyes can be different than the distance you hold your hook and yarn.

Double the Fun

Take your skills and your accessories to the next level with this chunky variegated scarf. Worked in double crochet, it will introduce you to creating consecutive rows easily and evenly. With a large hook in one hand and big yarn in the other, you'll accomplish a whole lot in very little time.

Crocheted Measurements
- Approx 9½" x 48"/24 x 122cm

Materials
- 14oz/400g or 220yd/200m of any super bulky weight wool yarn in a purple and blue variegated colorway (6)
- Size N/15 (10mm) crochet hook *or size to obtain gauge*

Gauge
8 sts to 4"/10cm over dc using size N/15 (10mm) crochet hook.
Take time to check gauge.

Scarf
Ch 21.
Row 1 Dc in 4th ch from hook and in each ch across—19 sts. Ch 3, turn.
Row 2 Dc in each st across. Ch 3, turn.
Rep row 2 for pat st and work even until piece measures 48"/122cm from beg. Fasten off. Weave in ends.

Tip
When purchasing the yarn for a project, don't forget to check the ball band! You'll find two numbers printed on the label. One is the color number and the other is the dye lot number. Make sure that all the balls you buy have the same dye lot number, because different dye lots of the same color can vary drastically.

Pillow Talk

You'll come full circle with this chunky crochet-in-the-round pillow. The crossed double crochet stitches will enhance the texture of the tropically toned yarn while also creating open decorative spaces at the center and on the edges for a hip casual look.

Crocheted Measurements
- Approx 14"/36cm in diameter

Materials
- 7½oz/210g or 180yd/110m of any super bulky weight wool and acrylic blend yarn in a pink, blue and yellow multi (6)
- Size L/11 (8mm) crochet hook *or size to obtain gauge*
- 14"/36cm round pillow form

Gauge
10 sts to 4"/10cm over sc using size L/11 (8mm) crochet hook.
Take time to check gauge.

Stitch Glossary
2Cdc (2 crossed double crochets)
Skip next st, work 1 dc in next st, then work 1 dc in the skipped st.

Back
Ch 2.
Rnd 1 Work 6 sc in 2nd ch from hook. Join rnd with a sl st in first sc.
Rnd 2 Ch 2, work 2 hdc in same st as sl st, then work 2 hdc in each st around—12 sts. Join rnd with a sl st in first hdc.
Rnd 3 Ch 1, work 2 sc in same st as sl st, then work 2 sc in each st around—24 sts. Join rnd with a sl st in first sc.
Rnd 4 Ch 3, *work 2Cdc over next 2 sts; rep from * around 11 times more. Join rnd with a sl st in first dc.
Rnd 5 Ch 1, work 2 sc in same st as sl st, then work 2 sc in each st around—48 sts. Join rnd with a sl st in first sc.
Rnd 6 Ch 2, hdc in same st as sl st, then work 1 hdc in each st around. Join rnd with a sl st in first hdc.
Rnd 7 Ch 1, sc in same st as sl st, *work 2 sc in next st, sc in next st; rep from * around—72 sts. Join rnd with a sl st in first sc.
Rnd 8 Rep rnd 4; working rep from * a total of 36 times.
Rnd 9 Ch 1, sc in same st as sl st, then work 1 sc in each st around. Join rnd with a sl st in first sc.
Rnd 10 Ch 2, hdc in same st as sl st, then work 1 hdc in each st around. Join rnd with a sl st in first hdc.
Rnd 11 Ch 1, sc in same st as sl st, sc in next st, *work 2 sc in next st, sc in next 2 sts; rep from * around—96 sts. Join rnd with a sl st in first sc. Fasten off.

Front
Work same as for back.

Finishing
With RS facing, sew back to front leaving an 8"/20.5cm opening. Turn RS out. Insert pillow form, then whipstitch opening closed.

Full Circle

Take to the slopes in this Andean earflap hat, beautifully striped in bright colors favored by the local artisans of that region. What you'll favor in this design is the beautiful bulky alpaca bouclé, which you'll use to master changing colors and finishing edges.

Sizes
- Instructions are written for one size and will fit most adults.

Crocheted Measurements
- Head circumference 21"/53cm

Materials
- 3½/100g or 140yd/130m of any super bulky weight wool and acrylic blend yarn in red (A), pink (B) and turquoise (C) **6**
- Size K/10½ (6.5mm) crochet hook *or size to obtain gauge*

Gauge
10 hdc and 10 rows/rnds (hdc and sc) to 4"/10cm over stripe pat using size K/10½ (6.5mm) hook. *Take time to check gauge.*

Note
When changing to a new color at end of rnd (or row), work to last 2 (or 3) lps that are on hook for last sc (or hdc), draw new color through the last 2 (or 3) lps on hook. Use new color to join rnd in first st (or ch and turn for rows).

Hat
Beg at top of crown with A, ch 4. Join ch with a sl st forming a ring.
Rnd 1 (RS) With A, ch 2, work 6 hdc in ring. Join this and all following rnds with a sl st in first st.
Rnd 2 With A, ch 2, work 2 hdc in each st around, changing to C—12 sts. Join.
Rnd 3 With C, ch 1, work 1 sc in first st, *2 sc in next st, 1 sc in next st; rep from * around changing to B—18 sts. Join.
Rnd 4 With B, ch 1, sc in first 2 sts, *work 2 sc in next st, sc in next 2 sts; rep from * around—24 sts. Join.
Rnd 5 With B, ch 1, sc in each st around, changing to C. Join.
Rnd 6 With C, ch 1, *sc in next 3 sts, work 2 sc in next st; rep from * around changing to A—30 sts. Join.
Rnd 7 With A, ch 2, *hdc in next 2 sts, work 2 hdc in next st, hdc in next 2 sts; rep from * around—36 sts. Join.
Rnd 8 With A, ch 2, *hdc in next 5 sts, work 2 hdc in next st; rep from * around changing to C—42 sts. Join.
Rnd 9 With C, ch 1, *sc in next 3 sts, work 2 sc in next st, sc in next 3 sts; rep from * around changing to B—48 sts. Join.
Rnd 10 With B, ch 2, work 2 hdc in first st, *hdc in next 7 sts, work 2 hdc in next st; rep from * around—54 sts. Join.
Rnd 11 With B, ch 2, hdc in each st around, changing to C. Join.
Rnd 12 With C, ch 1, sc in each st around, changing to A. Join.
Rnd 13 With A, ch 2, hdc in each st around. Join.
Rnd 14 With A, ch 2, hdc in each st around, changing to C. Join.
Rnd 15 Rep rnd 12 changing to B. Join.
Rnd 16 With B, ch 2, hdc in each st around. Join.
Rnd 17 With B, ch 2, hdc in each st around, changing to C. Join.
Rnd 18 Rep rnd 12.
Rnd 19 With A, ch 2, hdc in each st around. Join.
Rnd 20 With A, ch 2, hdc in each st around, changing to C. Join.

Left Earflap
Row 1 (RS) With C, ch 1, sc in first 12 sts, changing to B. Ch 2, turn.
Row 2 With B, hdc in 12 sts. Ch 2, turn.
Row 3 With B, hdc in 12 sts, changing to C. Ch 1, turn.
Row 4 With C, dec 1 sc over first 2 sts, sc in next 8 sts, dec 1 sc over last 2 sts, changing to A—10 sts. Ch 2, turn.
Row 5 With A, dec 1 hdc over first 2 sts, hdc in next 6 sts, dec 1 hdc over last 2 sts—8 sts. Ch 2, turn.
Row 6 With A, dec 1 hdc over first 2 sts, hdc in next 4 sts, dec 1 hdc over last 2 sts—6 sts. Fasten off.

Right Earflap
Turn hat so bottom edge is facing up. With back of hat facing you, sk next 20 sts, then join C with a sl st in next st.
Row 1 (RS) With C, ch 1, sc in same st as joining, sc in next 11 sts, changing to B. Ch 2, turn. Beg with row 2, cont to work same as for left earflap.

Edging
Turn hat so bottom edge is facing up. With back of hat facing you, join C with a sl st in first st just after left earflap.
Rnd 1 With C, ch 1, work 12 sc across back edge, 20 sc around right earflap, 20 sc across front edge, then 20 sc around left earflap, changing to B. Join this and all following rnds with a sl st in first st.
Rnd 2 With B, ch 1, sc in first st, *ch 1, sk next st, sc in next st; rep from * to corner of earflap, do not skip sts at earflap corners, cont to rep from * around changing to C at end of rnd. Join.

Rnd 3 With C, ch 1, sc in first st, *sc in ch-1 sp, ch 1, skip next st; rep from * around. Join. Fasten off.

Ties (make 2)
Cut three 50"/127cm lengths of each color. For each tie, gather three strands (one in each color) together and fold in half. From WS, insert hook into corner st of earflap, then draw center of strands through st, forming a lp. Pull the ends through this lp. Pull to tighten. Braid for 8"/20.5cm. Knot to secure, leaving rem ends free.

A Step Up

Shape up into quite the crocheter with these picot-edged classics that will have you increasing and decreasing in no time flat. Traditional baby fare, these booties also feature pompoms at the instep and drawstrings at the ankle. They may be small, but they pack a punch!

Sizes
- Instructions are written for size Newborn–3 months.

Materials
- 1 skein 5oz/140g (approx 398yd/363m) of Red Heart/Coats & Clark TLC Baby (acrylic/nylon) in #8881 powder blue sparkles or #8737 powder pink sparkle **2**
- Size G/6 (4mm) crochet hook *or size to obtain gauge*
- Two small safety pins

Gauge
19 sts and 21 rows to 4"/10cm over sc using size G/6 (4.5mm) crochet hook.
Take time to check gauge.

Bootie
Beg at back edge of heel, ch 22.
Row 1 Sc in 2nd ch from hook and in each ch across—21 sts. Ch 1, turn.
Rows 2–4 Sc in each st across. Ch 1, turn.

Ankle Shaping
Row 5 Work 2 sc in first st (inc made), sc in each st to within last st, work 2 sc in last st (inc made)—23 sts. Ch 1, turn.
Row 6 Rep row 2.
Row 7 Rep row 5—25 sts.
Row 8 Rep row 2.
Row 9 Rep row 5—27 sts.
Row 10 Rep row 2.
Row 11 Rep row 5—29 sts.
Row 12 Rep row 2.
Row 13 Rep row 5—31 sts. Mark beg and end of last row for beg of instep.

Instep Shaping
Row 14 Dec 1 st over first 2 sts, sc in each st across to within last 2 sts, dec 1 st over last 2 sts—29 sts. Ch 1, turn.
Row 15 Rep row 14—27 sts.
Row 16 Rep row 14—25 sts.
Rows 17–21 Rep row 2.
Row 22 Rep row 14—23 sts.
Row 23 Rep row 2.
Row 24 Rep row 14—21 sts.
Rows 25 and 26 Rep row 2.
Row 27 Rep row 14—19 sts.
Row 28 Rep row 14—17 sts. Fasten off. Fold the piece in half lengthwise, matching back edges of heel and edges of instep and toe. Whipstitch back edges of heel together. Whipstitch instep edges together from beg of instep to toe, then whipstitch toe edges together.

Cuff
Join yarn with a sl st in top edge of back heel seam.
Rnd 1 Ch 1, sc in same sp as joining, work 28 sc evenly spaced around ankle opening. Join rnd with a sl st in first sc—29 sts.
Rnd 2 (eyelet rnd) Ch 1, sc in first st, *ch 2, sk next st, sc in next st; rep from * around. Join rnd with a sl st in first sc.
Rnd 3 Ch 1, sc in first st, *sc in next ch-2 sp, sc in next st; rep from * around. Join rnd with a sl st in first sc.
Rnds 4–7 Ch 1, sc in each st around. Join rnd with a sl st in first sc.
Rnd 8 (picot rnd) Ch 1, sc in first st, *ch 2, sc in next st; rep from * around, end ch 2. Join rnd with a sl st in first sc. Fasten off.

Ties (make 2)
Ch 80. Fasten off leaving an 8"/20cm end. Weave in ends. Beg and ending at center front, weave ties through eyelets.

Pompoms
Plush pompoms make a fun finish for baby booties, hats, mittens, and just about any garment where you want to add a touch of whimsy. Here is an easy way to construct them. When you've finished making the pompoms, simply sew them to the insteps of the booties as shown.

MAKING POMPOMS

POMPOM TEMPLATE

1 Cut two circular pieces of cardboard the width of the desired pompom; cut a center hole in center of each. Then cut a pie-shaped wedge out of the circle. Use template above as a guide.
2 Hold the two circles together and wrap the yarn tightly around the cardboard. Carefully cut around the cardboard.
3 Tie a piece of yarn tightly between the two circles and remove the cardboard.
4 Place pompom between 2 smaller cardboard circles held together with a long needle and trim edges.

Around the Block

You know you're a true master of the craft when you've learned the granny square, one of the oldest and most recognizable of crochet forms. Here, a collection of vibrant pastel squares are joined together for a delicate baby blanket with picot edging. Striped borders modernize this sweetly old-fashioned design.

Crocheted Measurements
- Approx 25½" x 32"/64.5 x 81cm

Materials
- 5¼oz/150g or 410yd/380m of any DK weight cotton yarn in light blue (E) **3**
- 3½oz/100g or 280yd/250m in coral (A), lime (B), mint (C), apricot (D)
- Size E/4 (3.5mm) crochet hook *or size to obtain gauge*

Gauge
One square to 3⅜"/8.5cm using size E/4 (3.5mm) crochet hook.
Take time to check gauge.

Granny Square
Make 63 squares foll placement diagram for colorways for first 4 rnds. Rnds 5 and 6 for all squares are worked using E.
With first color, ch 4. Join ch with a sl st forming a ring.
Rnd 1 (RS) Ch 3 (always counts as 1 dc), work 2 dc in ring, ch 2, [work 3 dc in ring, ch 2] 3 times. Join rnd with a sl st in top of beg ch-3. Fasten off. From RS, join next color with a sl st in any corner ch-2 sp.
Rnd 2 Ch 3, work 2 dc in same ch-2 sp, ch 1, [work (3 dc, ch 2, 3 dc) in next ch-2 sp, ch 1] 3 times, end work 3 dc in beg ch-2 sp, ch 2. Join rnd with a sl st in top of beg ch-3. Fasten off. From RS, join next color with a sl st in any corner ch-2 sp.
Rnd 3 Ch 3, work 2 dc in same ch-2 sp, ch 1, [work 3 dc in next ch-1 sp, ch 1, work (3 dc, ch 2, 3 dc) in next ch-2 sp, ch 1] 3 times, end work 3 dc in next ch-1 sp, ch 1, work 3 dc in beg ch-2 sp, ch 2. Join rnd with a sl st in top of beg ch-3. Fasten off. From RS, join next color with a sl st in any corner ch-2 sp.
Rnd 4 Ch 3, work 2 dc in same ch-2 sp, ch 1, *[work 3 dc in next ch-1 sp, ch 1] twice, work (3 dc, ch 2, 3 dc) in next ch-2 sp, ch 1; rep from * 3 times, end [work 3 dc in next ch-1 sp, ch 1] twice, work 3 dc in beg ch-2 sp, ch 2. Join rnd with a sl st in top of beg ch-3. Fasten off. From RS, join E with a sl st in any corner ch-2 sp.
Rnd 5 With E, ch 1 (does not count as 1 sc), work 3 sc in same ch-2 sp, *[sc in next 3 dc, work 2 sc in next ch-1 sp] 3 times, sc in next 3 dc, work 3 sc in next ch-2 sp; rep from * around 3 times, end [sc in next 3 dc, work 2 sc in next ch-1 sp] 3 times, sc in next 3 dc, end sc in beg ch-2 sp. Join rnd with a sl st in first sc. Fasten off. From RS, join E with a sl st in back lp of any corner sc.
Rnd 6 With E, ch 1 (does not count as 1 sc), working through back lps only, work (sc, ch 1, sc) in same corner st, continue to sc in each st around, working (sc, ch 1, sc) in center st of next 3 corners. Join rnd with a sl st in first sc. Fasten off leaving a long tail for sewing.

Finishing
Using E, whipstitch squares tog foll placement diagram.

Border
From RS, join D with a sl st in back lp in 3rd st after any corner ch-1 sp.
Rnd 1 (RS) Ch 1, sc in back lp of same st as joining, *ch 1, sk next st, working through back lp, sc in next st; rep from * around working (sc, ch 1, sc) in each corner ch-1 sp. Join rnd with a sl st in first sc. Fasten off. From RS, join B with a sl st in 3rd ch-1 sp after any corner ch-1 sp.
Rnd 2 (RS) Ch 1, sc in same ch-1 sp as joining, *ch 1, sc in next ch-1 sp; rep from * around working (sc, ch 1, sc) in each corner ch-1 sp. Join rnd with a sl st in first sc. Fasten off. From RS, join A with a sl st in 3rd ch-1 sp after any corner ch-1 sp.
Rnd 3 Rep rnd 2. From RS, join E with a sl st in 3rd ch-1 sp after any corner ch-1 sp.
Rnd 4 Rep rnd 2. From RS, join D with a sl st in 3rd ch-1 sp after any corner ch-1 sp.
Rnd 5 Rep rnd 2. From RS, join B with a sl st in 3rd ch-1 sp after any corner ch-1 sp.
Rnd 6 (picot rnd) Ch 1, sc in same ch-1 sp as joining, *ch 3, sl st in 3rd ch from hook (picot made), sc in next ch-1 sp, ch 1, sc in next ch-1 sp; rep from * around. Join rnd with a sl st in first sc. Fasten off.

PLACEMENT DIAGRAM

ADBA	DCBD	ABCA	BDCB	ADCA	ECBE	ABCA	9
DBCD	ADBA	BCEB	ABDA	CDBC	ABDA	DBCD	8
ACDA	CBDC	ACBA	DECD	AECA	CBDC	ABCA	7
BDEB	AEDA	DBCD	ACDA	DEBD	ABEA	CDBC	6
AECA	EDBE	ADEA	BCDB	ACBA	EDBE	ADBA	5
CDBC	AEDA	BDEB	ADCA	EDBE	AEBA	DCBD	4
ABDA	DCBD	ACBA	CDBC	ACBA	BCEB	ACDA	3
DCBD	ABEA	ECBE	ABDA	BDCB	ADEA	CBDC	2
ADBA	DEBD	AECA	CBDC	AEBA	BCDB	ABCA	1

Color Key
A Coral
B Lime
C Mint
D Apricot
E Light Blue

The Granny Square

Granny squares are the most popular of all the motifs used to make afghans, sweaters, bags, hats, and more! The concept is simple. Each round consists of groups of three double crochets. After you finish the first round, you will have four corners. For every following round, you will work two double crochet groups in each corner, thus increasing the number of double crochet groups and the size of the square.

1 With the first color, ch 4. Join ch with a sl st forming a ring. For round 1, ch 3 (counts as 1 dc), working in the ring, work two more dc for the first 3-dc group as shown, then ch 2 for the first corner ch-2 sp.

2 To complete the round, [work 3 dc in ring, ch 2] 3 times. (Note: As you crochet around, work the dc groups over the tail of the ring or tail from the previous round. This way you won't have to weave them in later.) This gives you three more 3-dc groups and three more corner ch-2 sps. Join the rnd with a sl st in the top of the beg ch-3 (the first "dc"). Fasten off.

3 From the RS, join the next color in any corner ch-2 sp with a sl st. (Note: Always alternate what corner you join the color in, so joins are evenly distributed.)

4 For round 2, ch 3 (counts as 1 dc), work 2 dc in same ch-2 sp (this forms the first half of the first corner), ch 1, [work (3 dc, ch 2, 3 dc) in next ch-2 sp, ch 1] 3 times, at the end work 3 dc in beg ch-2 sp, ch 2 (this forms the second half of the first corner). Join the rnd with a sl st in the top of the beg ch-3. Fasten off. You now have four ch-2 corner sps and four ch-1 sps (one on each side).

5 Join the next color with a sl st in any corner ch-2 sp. For round 3, ch 3, work 2 dc in same ch-2 sp, ch 1, [work 3 dc in next ch-1 sp, ch 1, work (3 dc, ch 2, 3 dc) in next ch-2 sp, ch 1] 3 times, end work 3 dc in next ch-1 sp, ch 1, work 3 dc in beg ch-2 sp, ch 2. Join rnd with a sl st in top of beg ch-3. Fasten off. You still have four ch-2 corner sps, but now you have eight ch-1 sps (two on each side). For every round that follows, you will increase one ch-1 sp on each side.

Changing the Chains

No matter how hard you try and no matter what fail-safe measures you take, you will occasionally either have too many chains at the end of a row or too few. Please, don't think less of yourself. This happens to all crocheters at one time or another, no matter how experienced they are. So what do you do? Well, if the number of stitches is a manageable amount—say, for a scarf—it's best to unravel all that you've done and begin again. But if you are working with more than 100 chain stitches, convincing you to unravel them all is going to be tough. Unfortunately, if you've made a big mistake, there's no other remedy than to start fresh. But if it's a small discrepancy, here are some fixes that will solve these two most common problems.

Too Many Chain Stitches

When you finish the last stitch and find there is one or more chain stitches left over, there are two things that could be wrong. One, you crocheted too many chain stitches in the first place. Two, you worked two stitches into one chain stitch by mistake. First count the stitches to see if you have the right amount, then examine the row to see if you did double-team a stitch. (Note: If you have worked more than two stitches into one chain across the row, you should begin again.) To remove extra chain stitches, pull on the back loop of the chain stitch next to the foundation chain tail. Pull the tail through the loop, then pull the tail through the next loop. At this point you will encounter a knot from the slip knot. Untie this knot. Continue to undo the extra loops to the last crocheted stitch. To secure the tail, pull on it to close the last loop.

Too Few Chain Stitches

If you find that you've come up short, there are two things that could be wrong. One, you crocheted too few chain stitches from the start. Two, you skipped a chain stitch or two by mistake (one skipped chain is okay, but two is a big no-no, so start again). Just to make sure, count the stitches to see how far off you are. To add on more chain stitches, work as follows: With the foundation tail at your right, insert the hook into the bottom loop of the last foundation chain. Using the tail, yarn over and draw through a loop—one new foundation chain stitch made. Continue to make as many chain stitches as are needed, then fasten off the tail. Proceed to work the remaining stitches into the new chain stitches.

Make Them Last a Lifetime!

TLC for Your Crochets

With so much time, energy, and money spent crocheting your handmade masterpieces, you now need to know how to make them last and last. Nothing is more heartbreaking to a crocheter than a shrunken, misshapen, or pilly sweater, scarf, or hat. But all of these mishaps can be avoided when you put as much effort into cleaning and storing as you have into making them. Here are important guidelines that you should follow to give them a long and happy life.

Reading the Fine Print

Let's take another look at the ball band that you've been saving from the beginning of your project to see what important information this narrow strip of paper contains regarding the care of your garment. Here's what you'll find that will help you care for your beautiful crochets.

1 Fiber content (wool, nylon, cotton, etc.).
2 Methods of cleaning: dry clean only, handwash only, machine-wash, plus suggested water temperatures.
3 Methods of drying: dry flat only or machine-dry permissible.
4 Bleaching (permitted or not).
5 Pressing: suggested method, iron temperatures, or do not iron!

6 Dry cleaning (which solutions can be used to clean the yarn).

Cleaning

Before dry cleaning or washing your sweater, be sure to write all of the finished measurements of your assembled sweater in your notebook. If the ball band says that you must dry clean only, give the dry cleaner a check list that has what the fiber content is, what the recommended solvents are (if listed), and also the finished measurements. Also, request that the sweater be boxed rather than hung on a hanger (you don't know how long it's going to hang there before you get it back). Although you should feel confident that your sweater will be returned to you clean, you should also expect it to come back the same size and shape it was before handing it over.

If the ball band says you can machine-wash and machine-dry the sweater, follow the directions for the recommended soap, water temperature, washing cycle settings, and dryer-cycle setting and time.

With handwashing, it's all up to you. Just remember that if the water is too hot, there's too much agitation, and if the soap is too harsh, your sweater will shrink and the yarn will mat and pill. To wash with a little TLC, just follow these simple steps.

1 Fasten any buttons (this will help maintain the shape), then turn the garment inside out (this will prevent pilling).
2 Fill a sink with cool water, then add a mild soap that's recommended for delicate fabrics. Do not use laundry detergent.
3 Immerse the sweater in the soapy water. Allow to soak for fifteen to twenty minutes, gently swishing it back and forth. Don't pull on or rub the fabric; the less it's handled, the better.
4 Rinse in cool water three to four times or until there are no more traces of soap.
5 Press the sweater on the side of the sink to squeeze out the water until it's no longer dripping; do not twist or wring out. Lay it flat on a terrycloth towel, then gently but firmly roll the towel toward the opposite end to squeeze out even more moisture. Now it's time to move on to the directions for blocking and drying below.

Blocking and Drying

The two most important things to remember when drying a garment are: Dry it flat (to prevent it from stretching out) and dry it fast (to prevent it from getting mildewed).

Always dry sweaters flat on a terrycloth towel or sweater-drying rack. If you are using towels, change them often to speed up drying. To cut down on the amount of towels needed to dry a sweater, a great investment is the drying rack. It's made of mesh, which cuts down on drying time even more, and can be propped over a bathtub or sink and even hung from a clothesline.

Reshape the sweater with your hands, pushing trims into place and shaping the neckline, hem, and cuffs (just like you did in the original blocking). Use a tape measure to make sure the sweater matches the original finished measurements. If you are careful when drying your sweater, you won't have to steam or reblock it at all.

Place the sweater to dry away from direct heat (like a radiator) and sunlight, which can shrink the sweater, fade or discolor the yarn, and make the fibers brittle. However, the area should be warm and dry because a sweater will dry too slowly when the air around it is cold and damp. If possible, avoid washing on a rainy day when the humidity is high. Turn the sweater over as often as needed to allow both sides to dry evenly.

Ten Timeless Tips

1 Don't forget to wash your gauge swatch along with your sweater to make sure you'll always have matching yarn to use in case you need to make a repair.

2 Mending should always be done before cleaning, so the repair yarn will blend in.

3 The minute a spill happens, spot-clean your garment so the stain doesn't set in.

4 Always wash your hands before picking up your crochet. Skin oils can soil the yarn, especially if you are working with white or light colors.

5 Never hang a sweater on a hanger, hook, or back of a chair. This will cause unsightly "football shoulders," lumps, and stretch it out of shape.

6 Always fold your sweaters and stack them in a staggered fashion so they won't topple over. Store the stack in a cool, dry place.

7 To prevent moths, store in a cedar-lined trunk or closet, or simply tuck in a few cedar blocks between the layers of sweaters.

8 If you're short on storage space you can store your handmades in polyethylene plastic boxes made especially for clothing or blankets. Never store in cardboard boxes or the plastic from the dry cleaners. Wood-pulp fiber and polypropylene plastic release volatile gases that break down yarn fiber over time, discoloring it and making it brittle.

9 To air out a sweater, slip a pair of pantyhose inside the sweater and have a leg come out of each sleeve. Using clothespins, fasten the pantyhose toes to a clothesline (out of sunlight, of course). Leave outside for an hour or two. The fresh air will eliminate odors and fluff up the fibers, which will make it look brand-new.

10 Wearing a pin or brooch on a sweater can cause the stitches and yarn to stretch out and sag. To prevent this problem, purchase felt in a color that matches the yarn. Cut out a narrow rectangle as long as the pin back. Place the felt rectangle on the wrong side of the sweater behind the pin, then fasten the pin through both layers.